DANG IN THE MINE!

Abie Longstaff

Illustrated by **Julia Castaño**

OXFORD
UNIVERSITY PRESS

Letter from the Author

I've written over 40 books for children and I've always loved reading stories about horses. Did you know that some ponies worked underground in the coal mines? They had a very hard life and hardly ever went outside. The mine was a dangerous place and the ponies had to be strong and brave. I wondered what it would be like for a pony who was scared, so I wrote a story about Jem the pony, and her friend Charlie.

If you want to learn more about pit ponies there is lots of information at the National Coal Mining Museum. You could look on their website.

Abie Longstaff

Chapter One

Charlie wriggled on the wooden bench. Waiting, waiting ...
Clang! Clang! Clang!
At last, it was the end of the school day.

Charlie burst out of the school house and across the field.

He was sprinting through the orchard when he spotted a shiny red apple on the grass. Jem loved those! Charlie stopped, shoved it into his satchel and sped on towards the hills.

Charlie slowed down as he reached the side of the hill. There in front of him was a deep tunnel: the entrance to the mine.

'I'm coming, Jem,' he whispered. He squeezed through the fence and into the mine.

The sunlight vanished in an instant.
Trolleys clanked and tools tapped.

Charlie ran through the mine until he
reached the underground stables.

He ducked behind the first stall, hiding from the stableman. Charlie let out a low whistle and there was a whinny in reply.

'Jem!' he murmured, slipping into the pony's stall.

Jem was shaking. Charlie put his hand on her neck. He held it there, soft and warm, until she was still.

'Look what I brought you, girl.'
Charlie produced his treasure. Jem
snorted and gobbled the apple up, her
whiskers tickling his palm.

'I know you hate the dark tunnels,'
Charlie said. 'I wish you didn't have to
work here.'

'Oi!' said the stableman, spotting
Charlie. 'Stop spoiling the pit ponies.
Off you go!'

'I'm waiting for my dad,' said Charlie.

'Charlie!' Dad took off his cap and shook his head, sending dust flying.

Charlie laughed. 'You look like one of the ponies!'

Dad flung a sooty arm round Charlie. 'Have you brought me an apple too, then?' he said. He chomped the top of Charlie's head.

Charlie wriggled away, giggling.

'Let's go home, lad,' chuckled Dad.

Chapter Two

Outside, Dad stopped and took a deep breath in. He turned his face to the sun and closed his eyes. Charlie hugged him hard.

'I'm fine,' said Dad. 'But you shouldn't be in the mine. It isn't safe. Sometimes the firedamp builds up. That's a kind of gas, and it's really dangerous. One spark and the whole mine could explode. *POW!*'

Charlie flinched.

'Don't worry, son. We have Davy lamps. If the flame glows blue it means there's firedamp, and we get out fast.'

They walked on through the field, past the plough horses grazing.

At dinnertime, Charlie wasn't hungry.

'What's wrong, love?' asked Mum.

'Jem hates being underground,' he said. 'It's not fair.'

'I know you love the ponies,' said Dad, 'but they have an important job, pulling the coal trolleys. Before pit ponies, children did that work.' He put his hand on Charlie's. 'Jem will be all right. She just needs time to adjust.'

Charlie shook his head sadly.

'Charlie,' said Mum, 'you love making things. Keep studying, keep inventing. One day you might find a new way of mining. You have the power to change the world, you know, little by little.'

Chapter Three

After school, Charlie sat at the entrance to the mine, sketching on a writing slate.

There was a whinny and Charlie looked up. Jem was coming out of the tunnel pulling a trolley full of coal.

He whistled and Jem sped up to see him. The trolley wobbled on the rails.

'Whoa there!' The stableman glared at Charlie. 'You nearly had her trotting! This whole trolley-load could have come off the rails! This is no place for a child,' he snapped. 'You're not to bother the ponies again.'

Charlie turned and walked away before the stableman could see the tears in his eyes. He closed his fists tightly. He was going to change things, like Mum said. Little by little.

There must be a way to help the ponies, thought Charlie.

He began sketching ...

Three days later, Charlie showed his sketch to his teacher. 'So the coal comes out on this moving belt,' he said.

Mrs Adams nodded at him to continue.

'It comes out little by little, instead of in single big loads,' Charlie explained. 'That means it's not so heavy. It doesn't need ponies at all.'

Mrs Adams smiled and clapped! Charlie couldn't wait to tell Dad.

Chapter Four

After school, Charlie went to the orchard. He missed Jem. He hadn't been to the mine since the stableman scared him off. He searched the grass for the juiciest apple.

'I'll wait for Jem at the entrance to the mine,' he thought. 'I'll ask the stableman if I can give it to her.'

Charlie waited and waited for Jem to appear. Where was she? Was she hurt?

Charlie took a few steps into the tunnel and then a few more. He heard a jingling sound – maybe Jem was coming? Charlie walked on, further and further. He came to a fork in the tracks. Should he go left or right? A jingle-jangle came from the left, so Charlie followed it.

But when he reached the jangling sound, it wasn't Jem. A Davy lamp was hanging from a hook, metal tinging in the breeze. Disappointed, Charlie turned to go back. Only ... which way? He took one turning, then another.

Charlie heard a familiar voice. He rushed ahead, past a line of trolleys tipped over on their sides. Then suddenly he saw ...

'Dad!' Charlie flew into Dad's arms.

Dad shook his head. 'This area isn't safe!'

'I'll take you out,' said Dad. 'Stand back while Jack and I get this trolley upright.'

'Heave!' Dad and Jack lifted the trolley, but ...

'Whooaah!'

The heavy trolley lurched off the rails. It hit a wooden roof support! Tiny rocks rained down. Dad yanked Charlie back.

Creak!

The rock above them moaned and groaned.

'Get away!' warned Jack.

Charlie scrambled backwards.

Crash!

Charlie flung his arms over his head as the roof came tumbling down. His mouth filled with dust and his eyes streamed.

'Dad!' Charlie coughed out.

'I'm here!' gasped Dad. 'Stay still, lad.'

Charlie blinked and wiped his eyes. In the flickering light of the Davy lamps he saw a large jagged shape. A pile of fallen rocks was blocking their way out, with a big boulder right at the top!

Dad moaned. 'My leg,' he said. 'I think it's broken.'

'I'll get you out,' promised Jack.

He pushed at the pile of rock. He scrabbled and tugged.

'It's no use,' gasped Jack. 'That boulder won't budge. And the gaps are just too small to squeeze through.'

'Wait here,' said Dad. 'Someone will come.'

They waited and waited. Charlie held on tight to Dad. He watched the Davy lamp flickering yellow and orange and …

'Blue!' Charlie cried out in fear. 'The flame is blue!'

'Help!' they called and called. But no one came.

Jingle-jangle went the lamp, and suddenly Charlie had an idea.

He climbed up the pile of rocks and put his mouth to a gap. He whistled again and again.

'There's no point, boy,' said Jack. 'We're deep down. No one will hear.'

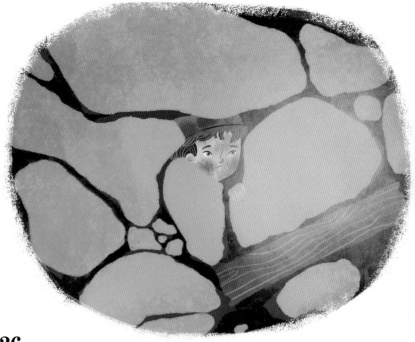

Charlie took a deep breath and whistled as hard as he could.

He heard the trotting of hooves.

'This way, girl!' called Charlie.

A soft nose appeared.

'Jem!'

Charlie reached his arm through the gap. He grabbed one end of Jem's rope, looping it round the boulder and out through a gap on the other side. Charlie tied the rope tightly to Jem's harness.

'Pull, Jem!' Charlie cried.

Jem pulled and pulled, her hooves slipping on the ground. The rope tightened. The boulder loosened.

'You can do it, Jem!' whispered Charlie.

The boulder rocked and ...

Thunk! The boulder fell off the pile!

Charlie climbed out and helped Jack and Dad through.

'Let's go!' cried Jack, hoisting Dad onto his shoulder. 'Before the firedamp explodes.'

Charlie felt his way along the rope to
Jem. She whinnied and nuzzled his neck.

'You were so brave,' Charlie whispered
to her as she led the way through the
tunnels ...

... and out into the fresh air.

'You did it, Charlie,' said Dad. 'You
saved everyone.'

'It was Jem,' said Charlie. 'I told you she was special.'

From that day on, Jem grew more and more used to the mine. She still whinnied when she saw Charlie, but she didn't shake in fear anymore.

Charlie told her all his plans. He was going to become an engineer, he said. That way, he really could change things.

One day, pit ponies would be replaced by machines, Charlie was sure.

And you know what?

He was right.

Historical Note

The first conveyor belts for mines were invented in 1905 by a mining engineer called Richard Sutcliffe.